The Lion Book of
Five-Minute Bible Stories

For Laura and David R.J.
For Renato and the boys O.T.

Text by Lois Rock
Illustrations copyright © 2004 Richard Johnson
This edition copyright © 2004 Lion Publishing

The moral rights of the author and illustrator
have been asserted

Published by
Lion Publishing plc
Mayfield House, 256 Banbury Road,
Oxford OX2 7DH, England
www.lion-publishing.co.uk
ISBN 0 7459 4757 3

First edition 2004
1 3 5 7 9 10 8 6 4 2 0

A catalogue record for this book is available
from the British Library

Typeset in 18/24 Lapidary 333 BT
Printed and bound in Singapore

The Lion Book of
Five-Minute
Bible Stories

told by Lois Rock

illustrated by Richard Johnson

LION
Children's Books

Contents

The Beginning of the World

The very first story in the Bible is about the beginning of the world.

Long, long ago — before the Bible itself was written down — this story was probably told by parents to their children, for generation after generation. Its message is clear: the world and everything in it belong to God.

IN THE BEGINNING — and this story is about the very beginning of the world — there was a great, big darkness. It was a shifting, shapeless thing, like a dark and stormy sea.

Then God spoke, and God's voice had to be obeyed: 'Let there be light,' said God. At once, the light came streaming through the darkness, clear and shining.

'Wonderful,' said God. 'I shall call the light time "Day" and the dark time "Night".'

And that, indeed, was the first day.

On the next day, God spoke again: 'Let there be a dome of blue to keep out the shifting, shapeless dark.' At once it was done, and there was space for a world under a huge blue sky.

In this way day two came to an end.

On the third day, God said, 'Let the water under the sky gather in great pools, with land between them.' God called the land 'Earth' and the pools of water 'Sea'.

God was pleased and spoke again: 'Let the earth be covered with all kinds of plants.'

From the brown earth came pale green seedlings. They unfolded their leaves and grew in the shape and size God wanted. There were grasses and herbs, vegetables and trees; flowers and fruits and thousands and millions of seeds.

As day three ended, God was very pleased with everything in the new-made world.

On day four, God called in a voice that rang to the highest heaven: 'Let there be lights in the sky: lights to show when it is day and when it is night; lights that change to mark the seasons of the year.' God made the bright golden sun for daytime and the pale moon for night-time. God also made the stars.

God smiled as the sun sank below the world's horizon.

On day five, God made all kinds of creatures. In no time the seas were filled with slippery fish and writhing octopuses; shy, scuttling crabs and astonishing anemones.

Birds drifted in the clear blue sky; others chattered and twittered and trilled and warbled in the tall green trees; still more dipped low over the white waves.

'This is wonderful,' said God. 'Listen, all you creatures, here is what you must do: have many, many young. Make your homes everywhere in the world I have made for you.'

On day six, God made all the other different kinds of animals:
there were goats and bears for the hills; otters and racoons for the
valleys; jaguars and tapirs for the forests and, for the grasslands,
elk and moose and deer and wildebeest. All the animals were
different. Some were fierce and wild; some were gentle and tame;
others were too shy to step out of their hiding places. 'And you
too must have many young and fill the earth,' said God.

Then God made human beings: boys and girls, men and
women. There was something about every human being that said,
clearer than if it had been written, 'Child of God.'

'My people,' said God, 'I want you to have many children and make the whole world your home.

'And listen: I am putting you in charge of all that I have made. Take good care of it, and the world will provide you with everything you need.'

In this way the whole universe was made. It was great and majestic and strong; it was also gentle and lovely and good.

On the seventh day, God stopped work. 'Every seventh day must be a special day,' said God. 'It must be a day of rest for everything I have made; it must be set aside as a special day for evermore.' ❧

The Garden of Eden

The second story in the Bible is about the first man and the first woman.

In the story, God makes a world that is perfect in every way. The man and the woman live in a garden paradise. Then temptation comes along: what else is there to discover…?

WHEN GOD MADE the world, God planted a garden in Eden. It was filled with trees, and they produced the most delicious fruit.

In the middle of the garden stood a very mysterious tree: anyone who ate its fruit would know not only good things but also bad things.

God brought the first man to the garden. 'Adam,' said God, 'I need you to take care of this place, and everything here is for you to enjoy. Just one warning: you must not touch the fruit on the tree in the middle of the garden. It will make you know not only good things but also bad things; then, in the end, you will die.'

Adam had no time even to think about forbidden fruit. He had his first job to do: naming the animals.

A little creature leapt down to his feet and miaowed. 'Hello, Cat,' said Adam. A larger creature stepped forward majestically. '"Big cat",' he announced. A third creature crept near on velvet paws. 'Oh,' said Adam. 'Another sort of big cat. Well, one can be "Lion", and this other one, "Jaguar".'

And so it went on. When all the animals had names, Adam began exploring. Then he sat down to rest. He went for a walk to places he had been before. In the end he sat down and sighed. 'It's not much fun on my own,' he said dolefully.

So God made a woman to be Adam's companion. Adam and Eve were the best of friends. Their days were completely happy.

One day, a snake came slithering along to the woman. 'Nice to sssee you,' it said, and it danced a swaying dance before adding: 'Sssplendid garden we share.'

'It's wonderful,' said Eve.

'Is anything off limitsss?' asked the snake.

'Only one tree,' Eve replied carelessly. 'God told us not to eat the fruit of this tree here because it will make us know not only good things but also bad things; then, in the end, we will die.'

The snake simpered scornfully. 'Silliness!' it said. 'Sstrange of God to say that… unlessss, God doesn't want you to be wissse. Sss! God must be jealousss.'

Eve looked at the tree. Its fruit was very tempting. 'Are you

sure there's nothing wrong with it?' she asked.

'Sure as a serpent,' it snickered. 'Try sssome.'

Eve reached out. She looked at the snake. She shrugged.
And then she took some fruit and bit into it. 'Amazing!' she said.
'I must share this with Adam.'

'Mmm,' said Adam, closing his eyes to enjoy the taste even
more. 'This is out of this world.' He opened his eyes. 'Ooh.
Doesn't everything look different?'

'Oh dear,' gasped Eve, turning away. 'We're both naked!'

She found a large leaf and tried to tie it round her. 'I think

I should cover myself a bit,' she said shyly.

'So should I,' agreed Adam. They spent the afternoon making simple clothes from leaves.

That evening, God came walking in the garden. Adam and Eve hid among the trees. 'Where are you?' called God.

There was no answer. God called again.

The garden was strangely quiet; the air, suddenly cold.

After a long silence, Adam stepped forward. 'I heard you the first time,' said Adam, 'but I hid because I was naked.'

'Who told you that?' said God sharply. 'Did you eat the fruit I said not to eat?'

'The woman you made to be my friend gave me some,' Adam replied.

Eve hung her head. 'The snake tricked me,' she muttered.

God was very sad. 'Now everything has to change,' God explained. 'Snake!' called God angrily. 'From this day forward you will crawl on your belly, and your tongue will lick the dirt.'

God turned to Adam and Eve. 'And you must leave the garden,' explained God.

In the world outside they found good things and bad things side by side, as they are to this very day. Adam and Eve had to work for all they needed: work till they ached, work till they died.

God set an angel to bar the way back into the garden, and the angel carried a sword that twisted in every direction, flashing like lightning. There was no way back. ❧

Noah and the Flood

The world God made good got all mixed up with badness.

In the mixed-up world, people began to quarrel and fight with one another. They didn't care a bit about God. They didn't care about how much they hurt each other. They didn't care at all about God's world.

LONG AGO, there lived a man named Noah. He was a good man and he loved God.

That made Noah different from just about everyone else in the whole wide world. People had grown wicked. Every day Noah heard people quarrelling; every day he saw people fighting.

One day, God came to have a closer look at the world and God saw all the wicked people. 'I'm sorry I ever made the place,' said God. 'It's become a disaster zone.'

So God made a plan, and Noah was part of it.

'I'm going to send a huge flood,' said God. 'Noah, I want you to build a boat. You are to rescue yourself and your family and a pair of every kind of animal.'

Noah set to work, building a boat of good strong wood. It needed to be big enough for his family and all the creatures. He and his family loaded it with hay and fruit and nuts and grain. Then they went to collect the animals and the birds. A long line of creatures came crawling and jumping, walking and running, leaping and flying.

'In you all go,' cried Noah.

Then the sky turned deep, dark grey. The billowing clouds began to rain. Water rose up in the rivers and the seas. It flooded the valleys and the plains; then it crept up the hillsides and right over the tallest mountain peaks. The bad old world had gone.

Noah and his loaded boat were all alone on the great grey flood. They floated on the deep for many days and nights.

But God had not forgotten them. One day, God sent a strong wind that blew the clouds from the sky. Slowly the water began to sink. Weeks and weeks went by, and then…

Berrr-ump. The boat grounded on a mountain top.

'Now what?' asked Noah's family, as they picked themselves up off the floor.

'Now we wait,' replied Noah.

'It's a pity we don't have a nice view,' said Noah's wife. 'There's nothing to see but water.'

Every day Noah went up on deck to survey the horizon. Every day he came clumping back down.

'Why not send a bird to go and look for land,' suggested his wife. 'It can look further than you can.'

Noah chose a raven. It flew away — and it didn't come back.

'That must mean something,' said Noah, 'but we don't know exactly what.'

Noah waited some more, and then he sent out a dove. It flew round for a while, but then it flew back.

'So you can't find anything better than this smelly old boat then,' said Noah, stroking it comfortingly. 'We'll try again in a week.'

This time the dove flew far away. When it came back in the evening, it had an olive leaf in its beak.

'So the land must be drying out somewhere,' announced Noah to his family. The following week, when he let the dove out again, it did not come back.

Slowly the water slid away. The mud glistened in the sun. Seeds awoke. Grass grew. It was time to open the door in the side of the boat.

Noah and his crew cheered and clapped as the long line of creatures hurried away, crawling and jumping, walking and running, leaping and flying. They were eager to build homes and raise families.

'And now for our own party,' said Noah.

As they celebrated, God gave them a promise. 'I will never

again send a flood like that,' said God. 'As long as the world exists there will always be summer and winter, a time for sowing seeds and a time for harvesting.'

The very last raindrops drifted away on the breeze. The sun came out. 'Look,' said God. 'There is the sign of my promise: a rainbow.'

Noah and his family and all the creatures looked at the beautiful colours arching across the sky, like the arch of a gateway to heaven. ஒ

The Tower of Babel

Sometimes people can be so proud of themselves!

This very old story from the Bible tells about some people who made a very clever discovery about making bricks. They were so proud of themselves they thought they could build a tower from earth to heaven.

God had a different idea.

WHEN THE WORLD was young, all of the people spoke the same language. Everyone could understand what everyone else said.

'Good day to you,' one might say.

'And good day to you,' another might reply.

'And are your flocks of sheep well?'

'Very well, thank you.'

In the beginning, the people were wandering nomads. They were always on the move from place to place seeking pasture for their flocks. Then, one day, they arrived at the great plain of Babylonia – a place where deep rivers flowed all year and where the trees were laden with fruit in their season. It was a good place to live, so the people decided to make it their home.

'Look how the river mud dries hard in the sun,' noticed one. 'It becomes as hard as rock. We could collect pieces of dried mud and pile them up to make walls.'

'More than that,' said another, 'we could shape the mud while it is wet so it dries into a perfect shape for building a strong wall.'

'Good idea,' they all agreed. And so they began making bricks.

'And look at this black slimy stuff that oozes up in places,' said one of the brickmakers. 'It's so sticky when it's wet that we could use it to hold our bricks together. Then, when the sticky stuff dries, the bricks would all stay put. They'd be unshakeable.'

'You know what,' said the brickmakers to each other. 'We could build homes from this stuff. We could build a city, and stay here for ever.'

'And as the brick walls are so strong, we could build a tower: a tower that reaches to the sky – to heaven itself!'

'Our city will be the most amazing thing in the whole wide world,' they agreed. 'We'll be famous! We'll be powerful. We'll be the greatest!'

So the building work began. Very soon, a great square tower had been completed. On top of that, they built another, and on top of that, another. Step by step the tower was reaching closer to heaven.

Then God came to see the city and its amazing tower.

'Just who do these people think they are?' said God. 'It's all because they speak one language and can understand each other. They are beginning to think they are superhuman. If they succeed with the tower – well, who knows what they will do next!'

God thought for a moment. 'I'll show them,' said God.

God's clever plan became clear as soon as the people next met to work on the tower.

'Pass me a brick,' said one.

'Don't insult my family,' came the unexpected reply.

'Are you plotting against me?' asked a third, who could not understand either of them. 'Are you speaking in code?'

God had given them different languages.

Soon the people began to divide into little groups to whisper and talk together, fearful of what the others were saying.

'We'll never be able to build anything now!' complained one group. 'We can't get enough people to understand what work needs to be done.'

'We're not going to work with people who just yammer on in gobbledegook,' sneered another group.

'Just listen to them!' laughed God. 'Babble babble babble. On and on and on.'

The people could no longer talk to one another. Soon different groups of them were to be seen setting out to find somewhere else to make their home.

Alone on the plain stood the unfinished tower of the people who babbled on: the tower of Babylon.

It was never finished. Never. ❧

Abraham and Isaac

Very early on in the Bible comes the story of Abraham.

In that story, God makes a promise to Abraham: he is going to be the father of a great nation, and through that nation, God will bless everyone in the world. Just one problem: Abraham doesn't have any children.

ABRAM SHOULD have been happy. After all, he was very rich. He had camels and sheep and goats and cattle, and slaves to take care of his household.

He also had a beautiful wife. Her name was Sarai and she was loyal and loving.

'But I don't have what I most want,' sighed Abram. 'Sarai and I cannot have children, so I have no son.' He sighed more deeply than ever.

In the silence that followed, God spoke to Abram: 'I have a plan for you,' said God. 'I want you to take all your household and go to a new land. I will bless you there: you will have a son, and then

grandchildren, and their children's children will become a great nation. They will bring my blessing to everyone in the world.'

Abram believed God. To the astonishment of his neighbours, he and all his family set out for the land of Canaan.

It was not yet his home. Abram and his household were always on the move, travelling from place to place in search of water and pasture for all their animals.

Life was hard. One day, Abram's servants quarrelled with his nephew's servants. The argument was so bad they decided to go their separate ways. Abram was left with the poorer land, where there was scarcely enough pasture for the animals.

And still Abram and Sarai had no children. 'We are really old now,' sighed Abram. 'I'm not sure God's promise was true.'

In the silence that followed, God spoke to Abram. 'I keep my promises,' said God. 'You are going to have a whole new start and new names. You will be called Abraham and your wife will be called Sarah. She will have a son and you will name him Isaac.'

The following year, Isaac was born. Abraham was delighted. He watched his child grow strong and healthy.

One day, in a moment of silence, God spoke to Abraham again. 'I know you love Isaac very much,' said God, 'but I want you to offer him to me as a sacrifice.'

A sacrifice? His own son? His only son? What was Abraham to do? He knew that some nations sacrificed children to their gods. Was his God like them? It would never do to displease God!

The next day, Abraham got ready to make a sacrifice and set off with his son and two servants.

When they got close to the right place, Abraham told the two servants to wait. 'Isaac can help carry the things we need from here,' he said.

The two walked up the mountainside.

'We've got wood and a knife and coals for a fire,' chattered Isaac, 'but where's the animal for the sacrifice?'

'God will provide one,' said Abraham darkly.

On the mountaintop, Abraham built an altar out of stones. He spread the firewood on top. Then he turned. He grabbed Isaac, tied him up and threw him on the pile. He raised the knife.

Then, in the silence, God spoke. 'Abraham. Stop. Don't hurt the child.'

Behind Abraham a ram kicked and struggled: it was stuck in a thornbush. 'That's the sacrifice!' Abraham laughed with relief as

he set Isaac free. 'God did provide one after all!'

Then, in the silence, God spoke to Abraham again. 'Now I know for sure that you will always obey me; and you know for sure that I keep my promises. Your children's children will be as many as the stars in the sky, as many as the grains of sand on the beach. They will bring my blessing to everyone in the world.'

Joseph and His Dreams

Abraham's son Isaac grew up and had two sons, Jacob and Esau. Jacob had twelve sons, but he loved two of them more than the others. They were the youngest, the sons of his favourite wife, Rachel. The fact that he had favourites caused a lot of problems.

JOSEPH WAS JUST seventeen. He felt like the king of the world. 'Listen to this,' he said to his brothers. 'I had a marvellous dream: we were all harvesting wheat and tying it into sheaves. Then my sheaf stood up straight and all your sheaves came and bowed down to it. Do you know what I think that means?'

'If you think we're going to do that to you,' sneered his brothers, 'you have another think coming. We're older than you.'

Later, Joseph had another dream. 'This one was really good,' he boasted. 'The sun, the moon and eleven stars came and bowed down to me. I think that's a special sign.'

'It certainly is,' muttered his brothers. 'It's a special sign of how arrogant you are.'

Even Joseph's doting father, Jacob, was not pleased. 'Don't you dare say things like that,' he warned. 'Stop dreaming and wake up to real life.'

Joseph swaggered around anyway. After all, Jacob had given him a special coat… the special robe a father gives to the son who is going to be the next head of the family. 'Because he thinks I'm the best,' he said to himself. 'And I am.'

So in a way, Joseph was partly to blame for what happened next. The brothers had taken the flocks to a pasture far away. Jacob sent Joseph to check that everything was all right with them.

'Oh, look who's coming,' they said. 'All alone. We could just get rid of him.'

When Joseph drew close, they grabbed him, ripped off his coat and threw him down a dried-up well.

They laughed and joked among themselves as he lay there, parched with thirst. As they laughed, they saw a line of laden camels striding through the desert. 'Merchants!' they exclaimed. 'We can sell Joseph. He'd fetch a good price as a slave.'

They pulled their brother out of the well and handed him over. When they finally returned home they told Jacob that Joseph was missing. 'Probably killed by animals,' they lied, trying to look sad.

In faraway Egypt, Joseph was sold to a wealthy man. He worked as hard as he could, but the man's wife accused him of wrongdoing. Because of her lies, Joseph was flung into jail.

The prisoners had little to talk about except their dreams. They liked Joseph because he was able to explain them.

He told one man he was going to be set free – and he was. He warned another that he was going to be punished – and he was.

The one who was set free was delighted, but he forgot all about Joseph. Then, one day, the great king of Egypt had two very puzzling dreams. 'There is someone in your jail who could explain,' the man whispered to the king. Hurriedly, Joseph was fetched out of jail, given a good wash, and brought to the palace.

'O king,' he explained, 'you dreamed of seven fat cows who were eaten by seven thin cows; then of seven full ears of corn that were eaten by seven thin ears of corn. The two dreams mean the same thing: there will be seven years of good harvests, then seven years of famine. You must find someone to take charge of storing food from the seven good years to last through the seven bad years.'

'I choose you,' said the king. Joseph became the second most important person in all Egypt.

Seven years went by. Joseph made sure lots of grain was put safely into huge barns. Then, all over the world, the harvests failed. When Joseph's family heard there was food for sale in Egypt, his brothers came to buy some.

They were brought to Joseph, and they bowed low to the

ground. They thought he was an Egyptian prince. Joseph recognized them at once. Could he trust them? Should he forgive them? And most of all, where was his brother Benjamin?

He asked them many questions, and when he found out that Benjamin was still alive, he demanded that they go and fetch him.

When at last they returned, Joseph welcomed them. 'Take plenty of grain,' he said. 'Sacks and sacks of it.'

Secretly, he told his servants to hide a silver cup among Benjamin's sack of grain. Then he accused him of being a thief.

'You must let him go,' pleaded the brothers. 'Our father will die of sorrow. He has already lost one of his sons. Punish one of us instead.'

Joseph wept. He knew they were sorry for what they had done so many years before and he was ready to forgive them. Then he told them who he was and invited the family to come to Egypt. 'God sent me here long ago so that I could keep you safe now,' he exclaimed. It was like a dream come true. ❧

The Baby in the Basket

Joseph's family all came to Egypt and made their home there. Years went by and the family grew to be a nation. Then a new king came to power: he knew nothing about Joseph. He didn't like having another nation in his country — not one bit.

THE KING OF Egypt frowned. He frowned at the floor. He frowned at the ceiling. He frowned at his courtiers. 'I've been thinking,' he said, 'and I'm not happy.'

The courtiers all tried to look helpful. An unhappy king always meant bad news for someone, and they didn't want the someone to be them.

'Those people that live in the land,' he said, 'the ones called Israelites. They bother me. What if they decide to gang up against us with some of our enemies? There are just too many of them. We need to do something. We need to stop them… breeding.'

'Let's make them slaves,' suggested someone helpfully. 'We need lots of slaves to build the beautiful cities you want, and slaves don't last long. The work kills them.'

'Good idea,' said the king. 'Make it happen.'

And so the Israelites became slaves.

But the Israelite people were strong. They didn't all die. In fact, the women still went on having lots of babies. Soon, there were even more of them.

The king scowled. He scowled at the floor. He scowled at the ceiling. He scowled at his courtiers. 'I've been thinking,' he said, 'and I'm not happy.'

The courtiers all tried to look helpful. An unhappy king always meant bad news for someone, and they didn't want the someone to be them.

'The Israelites are still breeding,' he said. 'So here is the new, improved plan. From now on, all of their newborn baby boys must be thrown into the River Nile.'

The king's soldiers followed his cruel orders. But one particular Israelite woman was determined that her baby boy would not die. For three months she kept him hidden in her home. Then she needed a new plan. Her daughter, Miriam, was eager to help.

First, the mother made a large basket. She covered it with tar to make it waterproof – like a little boat. She put the baby safely inside and carried it down to the river. There, among the reeds, she hid her little son.

'I'll keep watch,' promised her daughter, Miriam. 'I'll stay just close enough to make sure nothing awful happens.'

While she was watching, the king's daughter came along with her servants.

'This will be a lovely spot to bathe,' Miriam heard her say. 'With all these reeds around we can be sure no one is watching us... oh!'

She stopped talking and peered into the reeds. 'There's a basket in there,' she said. 'Can you go and find out what's in it?'

A servant waded in and brought out the basket.

'You'll never guess...' she began.

'A BABY,' exclaimed the princess. 'Oh, and he's crying.' She

picked him up and rocked him. 'It must be one of the Israelite babies… some clever mother is trying to save her baby boy from being killed… oh, he's gorgeous. I think I'm going to keep him.'

Miriam shyly stepped forward. 'I know someone who could nurse that baby for you,' she said. 'I could fetch her right now if you want.'

'That IS convenient,' said the princess with a smile. 'Yes please! I'd like you to go and fetch that person at once.'

Miriam ran all the way home. She came rushing back with her mother, who had never run so fast.

'Can you raise this baby for me?' the princess asked. 'I'll pay you, and then when he's a bit more grown up I'll adopt him.'

The princess smiled again. The little girl smiled even more. The baby's mother smiled the most of all. ❧

Moses and the Great Escape

Moses grew up as a prince in Egypt. He knew that his real family were Israelites and that all his people were slaves. One day, he decided to go and see for himself just how they were getting on.

FOR AS LONG as he could remember, Moses had lived in a palace. He was rich. Life was good.

'But I'm not truly Egyptian,' he reminded himself. 'My parents were Israelites. In fact, I would like to know more about my own people – even though they are only slaves.'

He was shocked to see them. The slaves looked so unhappy, so thin, so tired.

The Egyptians in charge of them looked mean. They shouted and flicked their whips. One slave master hit a man so hard he fell down.

Moses was angry. 'How dare you treat my people like that?' he said. He hit the slave master really hard.

To his dismay, the slave master fell down dead.

Moses glanced round. What a disaster! What could he do? Frantically, he buried the body in the sand and hurried away.

The next day he went back to the same place. He saw two Israelites fighting and told them to stop. 'Who are you to say that?' they replied. 'Are you going to kill us like you killed the Egyptian?'

Moses knew he had been seen. In fear for his life, he fled.

In the faraway wilderness he became a shepherd. Then, one day, he saw a strange sight: the thornbush in front of him was bright with flames... but none of it was burning. Moses went closer.

'Take your shoes off,' said a voice from heaven. 'You are on holy ground.'

It could only be God. Amazed, Moses did as he was told.

'Moses,' said God, 'I want you to go and rescue my people. Take them away from Egypt. Take them to a land where they can make homes for themselves.'

Moses protested. Moses argued. Moses fretted. 'The king will never believe me,' he said. 'I always stumble over my words.'

'You can ask your brother Aaron to do the talking,' said God. 'Now go.'

The two brothers went to see the king of Egypt. He looked at them through narrowed eyes and waved at them to speak.

'The God of the Israelites says this to you: let my people go.'

'What are you talking about?' sneered the king. 'I don't know anything about this so-called god.'

To his courtiers he said, 'Let's make life more difficult for the slaves. Make them work even harder.'

Time and again Moses and Aaron came back to tell the king God's message. Time and again the king sent them away.

God sent disasters to warn him. First the river turned blood red and then thousands of frogs came hopping onto the land.

Then came a swarm of gnats, then flies. Next, the farm animals all got ill and died. Then the people got horrible boils. The weather turned to hail. Swarms of locusts flew in from the dry desert and ate every bit of grass and leaf. Finally, the sky turned dark as night for three days.

'I'm still not letting anyone go,' said the king.

God spoke to Moses again. 'The people will go free. Tell everyone to get ready. Tell them to cook a lamb for a farewell meal, and to mark their houses with the blood of the lamb. In the unmarked houses of the Egyptians, the angel of death will stop and the firstborn son will die.'

When this disaster came, the king changed his mind. Moses led his people out of Egypt.

They had just reached a place of marshy pools and reeds when the king changed his mind again.

'I want my slaves back,' he raged. 'Send my fastest chariots and go and get them NOW!'

The Israelites saw the army and knew they were trapped between the enemy and the water. God spoke to Moses: 'Hold out

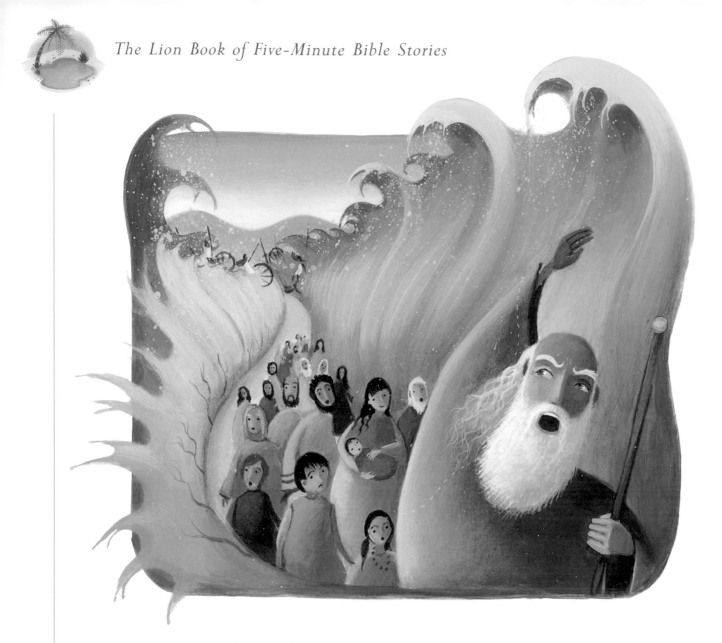

your arm.' As he did so, God sent a wind that blew a path through the sea of reeds. The Israelites crossed to safety. The Egyptian chariots all sank into the mud.

'God has rescued us,' shouted Moses, and all the Israelites began to celebrate. ❧

Samuel Hears a Voice

Moses led the Israelites out of Egypt. While they were on the journey, he gave them laws from God that told them the right way to live in the new land. Eventually they did reach the place and made it their home. When they kept God's laws, things went well. When they didn't obey God's laws, things went badly. Here is the story of one of the great leaders God sent to help them know right from wrong.

LONG AGO, in a little town perched among the hills, lived a man named Elkanah. He had two wives, as was the custom at that time. One wife was called Peninnah, and she had several children. Elkanah was very proud to be a father.

The other wife was called Hannah. To tell the truth, Elkanah loved Hannah more than he loved Peninnah, but Hannah was still very unhappy. The reason was that she had no children. Peninnah always made her remember that, and her unkind words made Hannah feel worse and worse.

One day, the family went to worship God at a place called

Shiloh. There was a shrine there: it was hung with the finest curtains, and in the innermost part was a beautiful gold box. Inside the box was a copy of the laws God had given the people in the time of Moses long before.

Old Eli was the chief priest of the shrine. He tried to tell people how to live as God wanted, but he wasn't very good at it. Even his sons disobeyed God – and they were meant to be priests as well.

Even so, Hannah believed that the shrine was special and that God would hear her prayers there. As she prayed, she cried and cried. The priest, Eli, saw her. He didn't understand what was going on and he was bothered at the way she was behaving.

'What's the matter with you?' he asked crossly. 'You look as if you've been drinking too much. Go away from here.'

Hannah looked up. 'It's not that,' she said. 'I'm just really unhappy, and I've been telling God all my troubles.'

'Oh,' said Eli, rather grumpily. 'Well, in that case, may God answer your prayers.'

Hannah went away, feeling a bit happier. By the same time the following year, she was a lot happier. She had had a baby, and she had named him Samuel. When he was a few years old, she brought him back to the shrine to show Eli.

'Do you remember me?' she asked. 'I was the woman you saw praying. Well, God answered my prayers. Here's the child I so longed for. Now he is old enough, I am going to give him to God, to do God's work all his life.'

Eli took care of young Samuel. Every year Hannah came back to visit, and every year she brought new clothes she had made for him.

Meanwhile, Samuel learned more about God and the right way to worship God. He really cared about those things. Eli's sons weren't at all interested. In fact, they behaved worse and worse.

One night, when Samuel was sleeping near where the golden box was kept, he heard a voice calling him.

That must be Eli, thought Samuel. He jumped up and went to

Eli, for he knew the old man was almost blind.

'You called me,' said Samuel, 'and here I am.'

'I didn't call you,' said Eli. 'Go back to bed.'

Samuel did so, but then he heard the voice again. He went running to Eli again.

'You did call me,' he said, 'so here I am.'

'No I didn't,' replied Eli, rather crossly. 'Go back to bed.'

The same thing happened a third time. This time, Eli knew what was happening.

'It is God who is calling you, Samuel,' he said. He spoke more gently than he had in a long time. 'If God calls again, say, "Speak, Lord: I am listening and I am ready to do what you want."'

God did speak again. God told Samuel that Eli's wicked sons were going to be punished. When Eli heard the news he was very sad, but he knew that God was right. He understood that God had chosen Samuel for something special.

As Samuel grew up, everyone began to see that he was a prophet: someone who spoke with all the wisdom of God.

Samuel became a great leader of the people. He helped them to make wise decisions and to live in the way that was right and good. ॐ

David and Goliath

Samuel gave the Israelites wise advice all his life. When he became an old man, the people asked him to choose their next leader.

'We don't want a prophet,' they said. 'We want a king, like the other nations. A king can help us win battles and make us strong.'

Samuel felt quite sure they were making a wrong choice. But he prayed to God, and God said to let the people have a king. God even told Samuel who it should be — a young man named Saul.

Things didn't work out as they should have. Saul did not do the things God wanted. God told Samuel to choose the man who would be king after Saul died: brave David. This is a story of how David helped Saul even after he knew he was going to be the next king.

THE SOLDIERS ALL LOOKED across the valley. Camped on the next hilltop was an army of Philistine soldiers, fierce and bold.

As the Israelite soldiers watched, two Philistines came striding out and stood alone on the hillside. The one in front held the shield for the other.

The Israelites gasped in fear. The main fighter was a giant of a man. His bronze armour glittered in the sunshine. He wore a javelin and a sword. His huge spear had an iron blade, sharp and deadly.

'What are you cowards doing up there?' shouted the giant. 'Who are you? King Saul's slaves? Come and fight me, Goliath.'

The Israelite soldiers huddled closer together.

'Here's an offer,' Goliath went on. 'If you lily-livered cowards can find anyone who can beat me, we'll all give in to you. But if I beat your little champion, you'll all lose.'

He laughed a wicked, cruel laugh.

As he went back to join the rest of his army, the Israelites whispered to each other. 'Do you dare fight the giant?' 'Ooh, no, not me. What about you?' 'Not a chance.' 'No.' 'No way.' 'No.'

The next day, the same thing happened, and the next. Goliath roared his challenge every day for forty days.

Among the Israelite army were three brothers from the town of Bethlehem. They had a much younger brother called David. He usually stayed at home looking after the sheep. One day, David's father told him to go to his brothers and take them some food from home.

When David reached the camp, he found his brothers lining up for the day's duties. Just then, Goliath came out of the Philistine army and shouted his challenge.

'Just look at him,' muttered the soldiers. 'King Saul has promised a big reward to anyone who dares fight him.'

David's ears pricked up. 'What's the reward?' he asked eagerly. 'I like winning.' Then he frowned, 'More than that, how dare that brute think he can beat us? God has promised to help us against our enemies.'

At that moment, David's eldest brother came along. 'What are you

doing here?' he snapped. 'Cheeky brat! Why aren't you at home looking after the sheep?'

'Just asking questions,' said David, and he sauntered off. To everyone he met he said the same thing: 'I'd fight him. And beat him. How do I get the chance to take up the challenge?'

When King Saul heard that someone was interested in fighting Goliath, he asked to see him.

'No one need be afraid of that hulking great soldier,' David told Saul. 'I'll fight him. And beat him. Please give me the chance.'

'But you're just a boy,' said Saul.

'I'm a shepherd boy,' said David. 'I have killed lions and bears because I have to protect the sheep. If God can save me from wild animals, God can save me from Goliath.'

'If you are really sure you want to fight,' said Saul, 'at least take my armour.'

David tried it on, but it was too heavy. 'I'll be better without it,' he said cheerfully.

He took his stick and a sling for throwing stones. He set off into the valley and picked up five stones from the stream.

'What's the stick for?' roared Goliath. 'Do you think I'm a dog?'

'You've got great weapons,' said David, 'but I trust in the great God of my people. So I'm sure I'm going to win.'

Goliath walked towards David. David ran forward, put a stone in his sling, whirled it round and threw.

The stone hit Goliath. He fell heavily. David ran forward and killed the fallen soldier with his own sword.

The Philistines ran away. The Israelites cheered. They had won! They had won! THEY HAD WON! ❧

Jonah and the Big Fish

This story is set in a time when there was a great empire to the north of the land of Israel: the Assyrian empire. Its capital city was Nineveh. People said that the Ninevites were the wickedest in the world.

JONAH WAS a prophet: he brought people messages from God. One day, God had a new message for him: 'Jonah, I want you to go to Nineveh. I have heard that its people are very wicked. Go and tell them just how bad they are.'

Jonah was not pleased. 'I'm not going to Nineveh,' he said to himself. 'The people of Nineveh don't deserve any warnings. I'm off somewhere else.'

And so he hurried down to a town by the sea. One of the ships in the harbour was about to sail to faraway Spain. 'I'd like to pay for a trip there, please,' said Jonah to the captain. The captain shrugged. A paying passenger? Why not?

Jonah settled down on the ship and smiled. Soon he would be as far from Nineveh as it was possible to get. He'd be so far away that God wouldn't be able to make him do anything.

The boat set sail. Jonah watched the land disappear. He watched the sky grow dim. He watched the stars come out. Time for sleep, he thought happily.

But when Jonah lay sleeping, a wind began to blow. The blowing became a gale. Soon a storm was tossing the boat up and down on huge crashing waves. 'We're going to sink!' cried the sailors. 'Throw the cargo out to make the boat lighter.'

All the time, Jonah was sleeping in a snug corner. 'Wake up,' shouted the captain. 'Pray to your God to save us.'

The sailors were getting more and more scared. 'This is a strange storm,' they said. 'It is the sort that means that someone here has done something very wrong, and their god is punishing them.'

They made everyone draw lots to find out who was the troublemaker. Jonah's name came up. 'You!' they shouted accusingly. 'What have you done?'

'I'm… er… running away,' said Jonah. 'From Nineveh. Well, from God actually.' He sighed. 'It is my fault,' he admitted. 'Throw me into the sea and you'll all be safe.'

'Well, we don't have to go as far as that…' said the sailors.

'No, you must,' replied Jonah, and in the end they agreed. 'Don't blame us, God,' they cried, as they heaved him overboard.

The storm stopped. The sailors were safe. And Jonah sank down, down, down, into the deep.

The end, thought Jonah. But just as he thought he could hold his breath no longer, a huge fish came and swallowed him whole.

Inside the fish, Jonah had time to think. 'This is no ordinary fish,' he said to God. 'This is your fish. Please save my life, and I will do what you want.'

The fish took Jonah to a beach and spat him out onto dry land. Jonah knew better than to disobey God twice. He went straight to Nineveh.

'Here is a message from God,' he announced. 'God has seen your wicked ways. God is going to destroy your city.'

'Oh dear!' said the people. 'We've been found out.'

'Oh dear!' said the king. 'That man is right. We must change our ways. We must say sorry to God. Perhaps God will forgive us.'

The king ordered everyone to pray to God saying how sorry they were for all the bad things they had done.

Jonah was very angry. 'I knew what you were up to!' he shouted to God. 'You always forgive people who say they're sorry.

Well, I'd rather die than see the Ninevites forgiven.'

Jonah went out of the city and found a place where he could be all by himself. He made a little shelter. God made a plant grow right by the shelter. It had big green leaves and gave Jonah some nice cool shade.

'Mmmm,' said Jonah, as he fell asleep. 'Zzzzz,' he breathed as he slept peacefully.

The next morning, a worm came and ate some of the plant, and the leaves wilted in the sun. 'This is awful,' complained Jonah. 'I'm dying of heat. And my poor plant is ruined.'

'Oh, so you're upset about a plant, are you?' said God. 'Well, if you can care about a plant, I can care about Nineveh. I love Nineveh. I love its people, I love the children, and I love the animals. That's the kind of God I am.' 🐋

Daniel and the Lions

The story of Daniel does not take place in the land of Israel. There came a time when the people of Israel were beaten by strong armies. Some of the important people were taken away to live far away, in the city of the great ruler of the conquering empire.

Darius claimed to be emperor of all the world – well, all the bits of the world that he knew about. He needed to find 120 good people to help him rule the empire. Among them was a man named Daniel.

DANIEL WAS the best of the bunch. Darius could see that easily. 'I must put Daniel in charge of all the day-to-day things that need looking after,' he said to himself. 'That way, everything will be done well.' He began making plans to give Daniel a promotion.

Soon, the other important people who worked for Darius heard of the emperor's plan. They were very jealous. 'We have to find some way to get Daniel into trouble,' they said. 'A nice bit of scandal would do. The problem is, Daniel is so very honest.'

'Just one thing about him is a bit, hmm, unusual,' said one.

'He's very religious; he's always praying to the God of his people.'

'Mmmm,' said the others. They smiled slyly. 'Very worrying.'

Then they went to the emperor. 'O Darius, may your majesty live for ever,' they grovelled. 'We, your chief helpers, have agreed on a new idea to help make sure that everyone in the empire is completely loyal to you.'

'Interesting!' said Darius. He rather liked feeling important.

'We urge your majesty to make a new law. For thirty days, no one in your empire shall pray to anyone or anything or any god. They must do this to show that they believe that you are greater – oh, far, far greater – than anyone or anything or any god. If they disobey, they must suffer a dreadful punishment… they must be

thrown into a pit of lions. And as everyone knows, your laws must not be changed.'

'Excellent,' said King Darius. 'I'll make the law right away…'

Daniel heard about the new law. He sighed. I still believe it is right to be loyal to God, he thought. So he went to a room in his house. It had windows that looked in the direction of faraway Jerusalem, where once his people had worshipped in God's temple.

There, as usual, he prayed to God.

Daniel's enemies were watching. 'Perfect,' they laughed. They hurried to tell Darius.

'O king,' they said, 'a terrible thing has happened.' They tried to look unhappy – which is a hard thing to do when you're brimming over with glee. 'Daniel, whom you trust so much, has disobeyed you. He knows about your new law, but we have seen him praying to his God.'

'Oh bother!' said the king. 'I should have thought of that. I already know about his quaint little religion. Well, he's so valuable to me that the law isn't really meant for him. We'll just not notice, and leave it at that.'

'O king,' said Daniel's enemies. 'You can't do that. You made the law – a law that can't be changed. You must punish Daniel, or everyone will think they can just ignore you and your laws.'

'No they won't,' said Darius.

'Yes they will,' said the men. They argued and argued, and in the end Darius knew he had better give in.

'This is all a bit of a mistake,' Darius muttered to Daniel as he was led to the pit of lions. 'But as your God has got you into trouble, perhaps your God will get you out of it.'

Armed soldiers threw Daniel into the pit and rolled a stone over the opening.

Darius went away scowling. 'I won't get any sleep tonight for worrying about Daniel,' he fretted. 'And no, I don't want a delicious meal. No, I don't want any jingle-jangle music and no, I don't want to watch dancing.' He sat up all night, just worrying about Daniel.

As the sun rose, the king rushed to the lion pit. 'Are you still alive, Daniel?' he called. 'Has your God saved you?'

'May your majesty live for ever,' said Daniel cheerfully. 'I'm absolutely fine. God knows I have done no wrong and sent an angel to save me from the lions.'

The king was delighted. He had Daniel pulled out of the pit. Then he scowled again. 'And now I'm going to show who's boss around here,' he said. 'I'm going to get rid of the people who wanted to get rid of you,' he said to Daniel.

All Daniel's enemies were thrown into the pit. At once, the lions pounced. ෂ

The Birth of Jesus

The people of Israel believed firmly that they were God's people. After all, God had made a promise to Abraham. Moses and Samuel had helped them to live as God's people. God's laws helped them understand right from wrong. Great David had won battles and, when he became the people's king, he started building the great city of Jerusalem.

After that, there had been bad times too: such as when the Assyrians destroyed half the nation; and when the Babylonians captured Jerusalem and left it in ruins for many years. The people of Israel began to believe that one day God would send a new leader... someone who would help them live as God's people: someone as great as King David.

IN THE LITTLE town of Nazareth lived a young woman named Mary. She was looking forward to getting married. That was exciting enough, but then something happened that was amazing and alarming all at once: an angel appeared to her.

'Don't be afraid,' said the angel – as if Mary could stop being afraid! 'God has chosen you for something very special. You are

going to have a
baby: God's own
son. You are to call
him "Jesus".'

Mary was astonished.
But she was utterly and
completely sure that what
the angel said wasn't true.

'I can't be going to have
a baby,' she said. 'I'm not
married yet and I know I can't
possibly be pregnant.'

'It is God's power that will
make all this happen,' said the
angel. 'Everything is possible for
God.'

'Oh,' said Mary. 'Then let it be so.
I am willing to do what God wants.'

What the angel said really was true.
Mary soon found out she was pregnant. Her
husband-to-be, Joseph, was very unhappy.

'She can't have been faithful to her promise to marry
me,' he worried. 'I'll have to call off the wedding.'

He fell asleep fretting about what was the right thing to do.
Then, in a dream, an angel appeared to him. 'You are part of

God's plan too,' the angel told him. 'God wants you to take care of Mary and her baby.' Joseph was a good man, and he agreed.

About this time, the emperor in Rome gave an order. He wanted a list of everyone in his empire. Joseph and Mary had to go to Joseph's home town of Bethlehem to put their names on the list.

They arrived to find the town was crowded. 'We must find a place to stay,' said Mary anxiously. 'The baby is going to be born soon.'

The best they could do was to share a shelter with some farm animals. In the low, dark cave, Mary had her baby. There was a manger for the animals' food, and it made a cosy cradle for little baby Jesus.

Out on the hillsides nearby, some shepherds were looking after their sheep through the long, dark night. Suddenly, an angel appeared. 'Don't be afraid,' said the angel. 'Tonight, in Bethlehem, a baby has been born: a king sent by God to rescue you and all people. Go and see: you will find the baby lying in a manger.'

Then, for one golden moment, the sky was full of angels. They were all singing for joy. It was like heaven had come to earth!

When the angels vanished back to heaven, the shepherds knew what they must do. They hurried to Bethlehem and found the baby, just as the angels had said.

Around the same time, some wise men saw a bright star in the night-time sky. 'It is a special sign,' they agreed, 'that a new king has been born.'

They followed the star many miles to the beautiful city of

Jerusalem. 'We are looking for a new king,' they said. 'Do you know where he is?'

The king in Jerusalem was a cruel man named Herod. He didn't want a rival! He'd bumped off his enemies in the past, and he was ready to do so again. But first he summoned his advisers.

'Our prophets have foretold that God will send us a king,' he said. 'Do they also say where that king will be born?'

'In Bethlehem,' they replied.

So Herod sent the wise men to Bethlehem, insisting that they return to tell him where they had found the baby.

As the wise men came near the town, they saw the star hanging over one of the houses. Inside they found Mary and the baby Jesus. The star had guided them truly. Here was the king! They gave their gifts of gold, frankincense and myrrh.

But the men were too wise to go back to Herod. In a dream, an angel warned them to return home another way.

An angel also spoke to Joseph: 'Take Mary and the child,' said the angel. 'Herod plans to harm him. Escape now, in the night.'

Joseph led his little family to faraway Egypt. There they were safe until the time was right for them to go home to Nazareth. ❧

Jesus Goes Missing

The people of Israel treasured the stories of their people in days gone by. The most important story was that of Moses. Every year they had a special festival — Passover — to remember the time when God helped Moses to lead the people to a new land.

EVERYONE JESUS knew in Nazareth looked forward to Passover. Families and friends always met together to share the special Passover meal. In fact, everyone who could went to the great city of Jerusalem, to join in the celebrations at the Temple there.

Jesus' parents went to Jerusalem every year, but Jesus wasn't allowed to go on the long trip until he was twelve. That year, as always, there was a big group going from Nazareth. The group felt like one big family, so Jesus didn't have to be with his parents every step of the way, and that was just fine with everyone.

They reached Jerusalem safely and everyone enjoyed the festival. The days rushed by, and all too soon it was time to go home again. Even so, as the group from Nazareth set off, everyone was still in holiday mood.

They walked for a whole day. As the afternoon shadows grew longer, Mary began to wonder: where was Jesus? She hadn't seen him since… since… well, since a long time ago. The group had got rather strung out, so she and her husband had to hurry around, backwards and forwards, asking everyone the same questions: 'Have you seen Jesus? Do you know where he might be?'

No one had seen him. No one had seen him at all that day.

Where did he get left behind? Mary worried. Why didn't anyone notice?

Inside she felt really upset with herself. Why hadn't she noticed? Then again, why hadn't her husband noticed?

Then she felt angry with Jesus: why had he let himself get left behind? And then she felt frightened for Jesus: what if he were lost and scared? What if something dreadful had happened?

Jesus' parents hurried back along the path, all the way to Jerusalem. They found a place to stay for the night so they could search the city the following day. They went to all the places they had been with Jesus, they asked everyone they knew. Three days went by and they just couldn't find him. It was getting desperate.

'Let's go to the temple again,' said Mary. 'That's where everyone heads for at Passover time.'

They went again to the huge temple courtyard. They threaded their way past the crowds to the white and glittering gold building in the centre. They walked into the court where men and women were praying and priests were hurrying into the holy place beyond. They walked round the outside of the building. They walked all round the edge of the courtyard, where there was a roof that gave some shade and people gathered to talk.

And then, at last, they saw Jesus. Mary almost missed seeing him – he was surrounded by a group of religious teachers, all grown men huddled around talking in a solemn and serious way. Jesus was asking them questions and answering theirs.

They looked very impressed at everything he said.

Mary rushed up. 'Why did you go missing?' she almost shrieked. 'Your father and I have been terribly worried. We've spent days trying to find you!'

Jesus looked surprised. 'Why did you have to look for me?' he said. 'Didn't you know that I had to be in my Father's house?'

Mary frowned slightly. What did Jesus mean? Then she remembered all her worry. 'Well,' she snapped. 'It's been a real nightmare for us, and you're never to do such a thing again.'

At once, Jesus got up to go with them.

Safely back in Nazareth, Jesus was as obedient as ever. He was even more interested in finding out about the old stories of his people, about the laws God had given in the time of Moses and the teachings of the prophets.

'He's quite a wise young man,' some people commented. 'And quite sensible. Not bad for an ordinary Nazareth boy who works in the carpentry trade.' ✌

The Hole in the Roof

When Jesus grew up, everyone in Nazareth expected him to do the same kind of work as his father, the carpenter. One day, he made a surprising change. He became a preacher and began to teach people about God and God's laws. The things he said seemed new and different: lots of people came to listen. It was also said that he could work miracles. Some people came to see him, hoping for a miracle.

IN THE TOWNS and villages near Nazareth, all the talk was of Jesus. 'People down in Capernaum are saying he's been working miracles,' said one. 'I'm going to find out more. After all, there's not usually much excitement round here.'

In the lakeside town, Jesus was in a house talking to the people who had gathered there. A number of religious teachers had come to listen to him, and they had taken the best places.

More and more people came – crowding round the door and out into the street. That was when four men came along, carrying their friend on his mat as if it were a stretcher.

The friend was paralysed: he simply could not walk. 'If only we can get you to see Jesus, perhaps you'll be cured,' said the four.

'If only,' said one, laying down his corner of the mat. 'But we're not going to be able to fight our way through this lot.'

The other three let the mat down too, to avoid tipping their friend on the ground! 'Have we come all this way for nothing?' muttered one. 'What a waste of time.'

'I'm not giving up,' said another. 'So Jesus is surrounded on all sides. Hmm… hmmm. Aha!'

'Go on, what's the idea?' asked the man on the stretcher.

'The roof is clear,' said his friend. 'Even the outdoor stairway to it is clear. So let's go up and make a hole in the roof. All we'll need then is ropes so we can let the mat down into the room… and we'll have Jesus' full attention.'

'Fun idea!' exclaimed the other three friends.

'Fun for who?' muttered the man on the bed.

It looked as if the people who owned the house used the roof as a place to store things. There was a coil of rope and a basket of tools. However, they hadn't taken great care of the roof, and the surface was worn and crumbly. The men found it easy to pull away the tiles and the plaster and make a gap between the rafters.

In the room below, people began to notice as flakes of plaster began to flutter down like snow. 'Do you think that ceiling's safe?' some people began to ask.

'Hmm, I don't know. Oh, look, there are people up there.

They must be fixing the roof. It needed repairs. Typical of workmen to turn up on a busy day like this.'

Even so, everyone wondered as the hole got bigger and bigger. There was a gasp of astonishment as the man was let down on his mat and set at Jesus' feet.

The people in the best places looked very put out. They'd given up their day to find out if this young preacher could be trusted, and now they seemed to be part of some village practical joke. What an intrusion!

Jesus didn't seem to mind. In fact, if anything, he seemed impressed at the men's efforts. They clearly believed that Jesus could help their friend. Jesus spoke to the man on the mattress. 'Your sins are forgiven,' he said.

The religious teachers looked very cross. 'How dare he say that?' they whispered. 'Only God can forgive sins.'

Jesus looked at them. 'What are you unhappy about?' he asked. 'I could say, "Your sins are forgiven" or I could say, "Get up off your mat and walk." So now you're going to see that I can forgive the man's sins.'

Jesus looked down at the man and said, 'Get up, pick up your mat and go home.'

At once, the man did. Everyone who saw was astonished. They could talk of nothing else.

They didn't even bother to find out how or when – or if – the roof got mended. ❧

The Storm on the Lake

Jesus chose twelve good friends. They helped him and learned from him as they went from place to place. Everywhere, Jesus wanted to teach people about God and how to live as God's friends.

ONE EVENING, Jesus and his friends came down to the lakeshore. Jesus had decided that they should go across to the quieter shore on the other side. As some of his friends were fishermen, they had a boat and knew how to sail it.

It was a calm evening. There were a lot of little boats out on the lake as Jesus and his friends set off. The air was almost still, with scarcely enough breeze to fill the wide, white sail. The sun slipped from the sky. The red and orange of the sunset faded to violet and grey. Soon the boat was just a dark shape on the inky water. Then it was night. Snug in a corner of the boat, Jesus fell fast asleep.

In the cool night, a teasing little breeze came skipping over the hills and swirled on to the lake, rippling the water. It seemed to sigh and vanish back to the hills. Then it came dancing back again, a little stronger, twirling like a lone dancer on the dance floor. Almost without warning, a hundred more dancing breezes came swirling down to join it.

At first the boat merely picked up speed, creaming through the water as the sail billowed. Then it began to rock up and down, up and down on the gently cresting waves. The fishermen looked at each other anxiously. They knew how quickly the weather could change, and they were right in the

middle of the lake, with a long way to any shore.

'Nearest harbour is over there,' said one curtly. 'Turn the boat round.'

But then, all at once, came the storm. The waves began to lift and break, lift and break again. They tossed the boat on curling crests and flung it deep into the troughs. The spray splattered into the boat, and water pooled and gurgled in the bottom.

'Wake up, Jesus, wake up!' shouted one of the friends. 'We're going to die out here! Don't you care?'

Jesus woke up. He looked around sleepily. He didn't seem the least bit alarmed. 'Come on, we need help!' yelled someone. 'We've got to get this sail down or we'll be blown over.'

Jesus stood up in the boat. He raised a hand, but in a gentle way. Then he spoke to the wind. 'Be quiet!' he said. Then he looked down at the angry waves. 'Be still!' he whispered.

All at once, the wind died down and shyly blew away. The waves went flat and the lake shimmered softly. In the east the dark clouds were edged with gold.

Jesus turned to his friends. 'Why

are you scared?' he said calmly. 'Have you no faith?'

They looked at one another, astonished at all that had happened. Then Jesus lay down again, and seemed to fall asleep in a moment. The men hoisted the sail and steered the boat to shore.

Among the friends was one who hardly ever got in a boat. He felt completely bewildered. 'I really thought that storm was going to drown us,' he whispered to one of the fishermen. 'It wasn't just me who was scared, was it?'

'No,' came the reply. 'It was really bad. It was the worst storm I've ever seen. I'm amazed we came through it.'

'How do you think Jesus calmed it all down?' whispered a third.

'No idea,' the others shrugged.

They all looked towards Jesus, their eyes round with wonder.

'There must be something more to him than we really understand,' they said. ๑

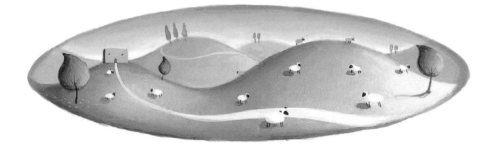

The Lost Sheep

Jesus spent a lot of time teaching and preaching. When he did so, he often told stories with a special meaning – parables. Here is one.

ONE DAY, as on so many days, a crowd of people came to hear Jesus speak. There were all kinds of people in the crowd.

Some of the people who came were very religious. They were the kind of people who studied hard to make sure they understood God's laws. They were decent people, who really tried to do what they thought was right. Unfortunately, some of them had grown rather proud of themselves and they looked down on people who did wrong things.

Some of the people who came to see Jesus were not very religious. In fact, there were a great many in the crowd who had a reputation for doing wrong things. They seemed to like Jesus, and that was probably because he made them feel welcome.

'Well,' grumbled the religious people, 'what kind of teacher can Jesus be if he has friends like THEM? By spending so much time with them, he's making himself as bad as they are!'

Jesus knew what they were saying about him, and he told them this story:

'Imagine that you're a shepherd,' he said, 'a shepherd with one hundred sheep.'

A good number, the listeners thought, nice size of flock.

'Imagine,' Jesus continued, 'that one day you lose a sheep.'

Ninety-nine left, thought the listeners. Still a good flock but, ooh, how annoying to lose one.

'What do you do?' asked Jesus.

'Find the lost sheep!' called someone in the crowd. 'Leave someone else to look after the flock. There's always a couple of children perfectly able to do that!'

'Of course,' said Jesus. 'You leave the rest of the sheep safely nibbling away in the pasture and you go and find that lost sheep.'

'And you don't give up!' called a shepherd.

'Those runaway sheep can go a long way,' added another. 'You have to keep looking. I've walked miles sometimes. You can't get a paid farmhand to put in that kind of effort, I can tell you!'

'Exactly,' said Jesus. 'Every good shepherd knows that they'd go looking and looking until they found their lost sheep. Then they'd pick it up and carry it home. And what do you think they'd do then?'

'Have a party,' called the shepherd. 'Get all your friends round.'

'You'd organize a big celebration,' agreed Jesus. 'And that's important to remember. Because that's a bit like what happens in heaven when some wrongdoer makes that big change. When a wrongdoer finally sees that they're making a mess of their life and decides to put things right, you can almost hear the angels cheering.'

'Good story!' called out some of Jesus' listeners. They recognized that Jesus was talking about them.

'Good understanding of the hard work shepherds do,' nodded some of the farming people.

'Mad,' muttered some of the religious leaders. 'He's mad, bad and quite probably dangerous.'

It was sad but true: Jesus and the religious leaders were not getting on together. But other people were flocking to him like sheep to a shepherd. ❧

The Good Samaritan

This story is one of the most famous parables that Jesus told. It makes people think about the right way to treat one another.

JESUS COULD see the man coming. He could see the man's smile: a little bit smug and a little bit smarmy. He could see the man's prayer shawl with its extra-long tassels… the telltale sign of a man who thought he was religious.

'Good morning, Teacher,' he said to Jesus. 'As you can see, I am a teacher of the laws of God myself. Having heard of your wisdom, I wanted to know your answer to this very important question: What must I do to win eternal life?'

'Well, you've read the holy books of our people,' replied Jesus. 'What do they tell us?'

'These are the two greatest commandments,' said the man. He put on his religious voice and recited: "Love the Lord your God with all your heart, with all your soul, with all your strength and with all your mind. Love your neighbour as you love yourself."'

'Quite right,' said Jesus. 'Do that and you will live.'

The man frowned. Jesus hadn't told him anything. He must think of another question if he was going to find out more about Jesus' teaching or – to put it more accurately – if he was going to find out more about what was wrong with Jesus' teaching. 'Well, who is my neighbour?' he asked.

Jesus told a story. 'There was once a man who was travelling from Jerusalem to Jericho. He was on the lonely road that winds down through the bare hills of the wilderness. Suddenly, robbers came leaping down from their hiding place. They grabbed him, punched him to the ground, snatched his money and kicked him senseless. Then they ran off, leaving him half dead.'

The man shuddered. There were tales of those kinds of attacks every week. It made an honest man like him afraid to go out.

Jesus continued. 'It just so happened that a priest from the Temple was going the same way. He saw the man but he didn't want to have anything to do with him. After all... he might be dead. Trying hard to look away, he hurried by on the far side of the road.

'Next came a helper from the same Temple, a Levite. He saw the man and went closer to look at him. I can't deal with this, he thought to himself, and he too hurried on.

'Then a third man came by,' said Jesus. 'A Samaritan.'

Jesus' listener raised his eyebrows. Samaritans had strange ideas about religion. Not only strange ideas… wrong ideas, as far as all the teachers of the Law could work out.

'The Samaritan saw the man,' said Jesus, 'and felt sorry for him. He walked over and carefully cleaned the man's wounds before wrapping them in bandages. Then he lifted the man onto

his own donkey and led him to an inn. There, he took good care of him.

'The next day he had to travel on, but before he left, he dug into his purse and brought out two silver coins, which he gave to the innkeeper. "Take care of this man for me," he said. "If it costs you more than this, I will pay you when I come back this way."'

Jesus smiled at the teacher of the Law. 'So what do you think: which of the three passers-by acted like a neighbour to the man who was attacked?'

'It's obvious,' said the man. He made a face at having to say anything nice about a Samaritan. 'The one who was kind to him.'

Jesus replied: 'Then you go and do the same.' ❧

Jesus in Jerusalem

Jesus knew that he had chosen a difficult path. From the time he became a preacher, he knew that teaching people about God's love and forgiveness would lead to problems with the religious authorities.

IT WAS A BRIGHT spring day. The road to Jerusalem was crowded. It was just a few days to the great festival of Passover – the festival that celebrated the time when God had led the people to freedom, long ago. Everyone wanted to be in Jerusalem for the occasion and to worship God in the Temple.

'We must go to Jerusalem too,' said Jesus to his friends. He told them where they could go to fetch a donkey so he could ride the last few miles.

As the donkey clip-clopped its way forward, people on foot moved aside. 'It's Jesus,' someone whispered. 'It's not usual for him to ride anywhere. Perhaps this visit is going to be something special.'

'He looks a bit like a king riding in to claim the city and the throne,' said another. 'Only, of course, a king would have a horse. And an army.'

'Yes, but maybe with crowds of people on his side he's going to show who's in charge in Jerusalem,' added another. 'No one likes that Roman governor, Pontius Pilate.'

There came a shout, loud and clear: 'God bless the king who comes in God's name.' Suddenly everyone joined in. 'God bless the king, God bless the king!'

Some people swept the cloaks from their shoulders and laid them down grandly in front of the donkey. Others cut branches from the palm trees that lined the road and waved them like banners. 'Hooray,' people were shouting, and they began to dance and to chant slogans about God's chosen king. There was a hint of revolution in the air.

Once he reached the city, Jesus went to the Temple. Inside the great courtyard everyone was getting ready for the festival. What a din they made! Stallholders were selling animals needed for the festival sacrifices; others were changing everyday money into the special Temple money people needed to make their offerings. Jesus could hear shouting and arguing — and no wonder: the stallholders were charging ridiculous prices. It was so unfair.

Suddenly Jesus was angry. He began pushing stalls over and driving the sellers away. 'You're no better than thieves,' he shouted. 'This is meant to be God's house.'

Coins jangled to the ground and a huddle of lambs stampeded round the courtyard. In a whirr of wings a crowd of doves fluttered to the sky, while people shrieked in fear and anger.

The noise brought the priests and the teachers of the law hurrying out of the temple building. 'What is the cause of all this?' they wanted to know. When they found out that it was Jesus, they were angrier still. 'We have to get rid of this man,' they muttered to themselves. 'We have to do so quickly, before he causes any more trouble, either with his mad stories or with his mad followers going on the rampage.' They began to make their plans.

In the end, it was all too easy. One of Jesus' friends, Judas Iscariot, decided to betray his master. He went to the priests secretly and struck a bargain. For thirty silver coins, he agreed to let them know when and where they could find Jesus alone.

Jesus seemed to know what was going on. He was very sad as he and his friends met to celebrate the Passover meal together.

He broke the bread for them all to share. 'Eat this,' he said. 'This is my body, which is broken for you. When you eat bread like this, remember me.'

After that he shared the cup of wine. 'This is the cup of God's new agreement,' he said. 'The agreement will be made final when my blood is shed. When you drink wine like this, remember me.'

Then they all sang a hymn and went to an olive grove not far from the city. Jesus went off by himself into the dark shadows to pray.

Judas had already slipped away. He came back while it was still night leading a band of soldiers.

Roughly they grabbed Jesus and arrested him. Jesus' other friends ran for their lives.

The soldiers took Jesus to the priests, and they put him on trial – questioning, insulting, blaming. People came and told lies about him. They claimed that he had said wrong and disrespectful things about God. They claimed that Jesus deserved to die.

The priests' minds were already made up, and in the morning, they took Jesus to the Roman governor, Pontius Pilate. Pilate didn't care a thing about their religion, they knew that much, but they had to persuade him to allow the death penalty. 'He is a dangerous rebel,' they claimed. 'You must get rid of him.'

The Roman governor was perplexed. He had seen plenty of rebels in his time, and Jesus didn't look like a troublemaker as far as he was concerned. But the priests had done their work well, and the crowd that gathered was there for a purpose.

They were waiting as Pilate came to the balcony of his residence. At Passover, it was the custom for him to set a prisoner free. 'Would you like me to set Jesus free?' he asked. 'No, free Barabbas,' they shouted. Barabbas was a terrorist and a murderer. 'What shall I do with this man?' asked Pilate, pointing to Jesus.

'Crucify him, crucify him,' they shouted.

Pilate knew better than to argue with the crowd.

'Take him away,' he said to the soldiers.

Whatever Jesus had dreamed of doing, it seemed that it was all over. ॐ

The Story of the Cross

One thing that all soldiers have to learn to do is to carry out orders. They didn't know much about Jesus: it wasn't their business to know anything about him.

ON A FRIDAY in spring, long ago, the Roman soldiers in Jerusalem had to execute three prisoners. One of them was called Jesus. 'What's he done, then?' asked the officer. 'He can't be one of those anti-Roman terrorists or I'd have heard more about him.'

'No, he's a religious nut,' said one of the men. 'The bigwigs at the Temple here don't like him for some reason. Look, here's the notice to be pinned above him: 'This is the king of the Jews.' Those people are always dreaming of having a king to set them free. Well, this man can't be him, even if he thought he was.'

They took their prisoners outside the city, to a place called 'Golgotha', which means 'the Skull'. There they crucified them, nailing them to crosses of wood that they left planted in the ground.

'That Jesus had a decent tunic,' said the soldiers. 'Let's not rip it up; we can play dice and the winner can have it whole.'

As the soldiers gambled at the foot of the cross, the crowds edged nearer, jeering at Jesus. 'So, you thought you were God's chosen king, did you?' they called. 'Go on – show how powerful you are now! Save yourself if you can.'

One of the other prisoners was angry too. 'Yeah, get us out of this,' he snarled.

'Leave him alone,' said the other. 'We know why we're in this kind of trouble. Jesus didn't do anything wrong.' Then he looked at Jesus. 'Remember me, won't you?' he said.

Jesus nodded. 'Today you will be in paradise with me,' he said.

But to the men on the cross, paradise seemed very far away. In fact, the whole world seemed to be under a strange cloud. At noon, the sun stopped shining and it became as dark as night. At three o'clock Jesus spoke in a loud voice: 'Father, in your hands I place my spirit.' Then he died.

The Roman officer was puzzled. 'That Jesus was truly a good man,' he admitted. 'Son of God, some people are saying. I could believe that.' He shrugged. He'd only been following orders.

Those of Jesus' friends who had gathered to watch began to walk away. They had believed so much in Jesus and his teaching. Now it was all over. There was no point in going on hoping for some kind of miracle.

Only one man was brave enough to go and ask Pilate for Jesus' body. Joseph of Arimathea was a secret follower of Jesus. He also had enough money to have his own tomb already prepared. He arranged for the body to be carried away and laid inside the low cave. Then he asked for the heavy stone door to be rolled shut.

The sun began to set. Friday was ending, and the sabbath was beginning. Jesus' friends had to respect the weekly day of rest, so they went back to where they were staying.

Very early on Sunday morning some of the women who had followed Jesus went back to the tomb to prepare the body for a proper burial. 'Do you think we'll be able to move the door?' they asked. 'It's very heavy.'

When they reached the tomb, the door was open. Two figures in shining bright clothes stood there. 'Why are you looking among the dead for one who is alive?' they asked the women. 'He is not here. He is risen.'

The women were amazed. They ran to tell the other friends. Something strange had happened for sure… but could Jesus be alive? Surely that kind of thing could never happen!

Over the next few days, they actually saw him. They touched him. They ate with him. They listened to what he had to say. Jesus

wanted them to understand the meaning of all that had happened through his life, and the meaning of his death and resurrection.

Through it all, Jesus had shown people how much God loves them. Now it was their turn to tell the whole world the same good news: the news that God welcomes people as if they were long-lost friends.

The news that nothing, absolutely nothing – not even death itself – can cut people off from the everlasting love of God. ❧